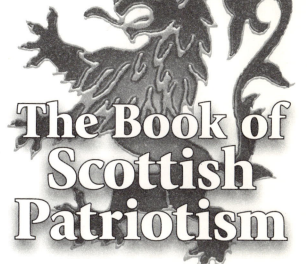

The Book of Scottish Patriotism

Here's tae us, Wha's like us?

Crombie Jardine
PUBLISHING LIMITED

Unit 17, 196 Rose Street, Edinburgh EH2 4AT
www.crombiejardine.com

This edition was first published by
Crombie Jardine Publishing Limited in 2005

ISBN 1-905102-29-1

Concept and compilation by Crombie Jardine
Designed by www.mrstiffy.co.uk
Printed & bound in Great Britain by
William Clowes Ltd, Beccles, Suffolk

CONTENTS

INTRODUCTION

HERE'S TAE US! WHA'S LIKE US?

The average Englishman gets ready for work in the morning and dons his raincoat – an item patented by the chemist Charles Macintosh of Glasgow (Scotland).

On his way to the office he drives along the English lane, surfaced by John Macadam of Ayr (Scotland), in an English car fitted with tyres developed by John Boyd Dunlop of Dreghorn (Scotland).

When he arrives at the office, his secretary brings him the mail bearing adhesive stamps, invented by John Chalmers of Dundee (Scotland).

Throughout the day he uses the telephone,
invented by Alexander Graham Bell,
born in Edinburgh (Scotland).

He returns home tired and wondering if there's
a conspiracy going on. He opens the front
door and surveys the pristine hallway where
the home help has finished using the vacuum
cleaner, the design for which was patented
by Scottish-born Hubert Cecil Booth.

He heads for the safety of his study where he
switches on the television, pioneered by John Logie
Baird of Helensburgh (Scotland). The first thing he
hears is a news item about the U.S. Navy, founded
by John Paul Jones of Kirkbean (Scotland). He
flicks through the channels to see what else is on
only to be bombarded by Scots all round, from old
episodes of Dr. Finlay's Casebook to Rab C. Nesbitt.

In disgust he turns and scans his bookshelves and what does he find? A leather-bound edition of An Inquiry into the Nature and Causes of the Wealth of Nations by Adam Smith, the Scottish economist and philosopher... Kidnapped and Treasure Island by the novelist and poet Robert Louis Stevenson, born in Edinburgh (Scotland)... The Waverley Novels by the writer, poet and great Scottish patriot Sir Walter Scott... various Sherlock Holmes mysteries by Sir Arthur Conan Doyle, born in Edinburgh (Scotland)... The Kilmarnock Edition of the poems of one of Scotland's all time great poets, Robert Burns... Coral Island by the prolific Scottish writer R.M. Ballantyne...

In search of comfort he turns frantically to the Bible, only to find that the first man mentioned in the good book is a Scot – King James VI – who authorized its translation.

Nowhere can the Englishman go to escape the inventiveness of the Scots:

He could take to drink but the Scots
make the best in the world.

He could take a rifle and end it all but
the breech-loading rifle was invented by
Patrick Ferguson of Pitfours (Scotland).

If he escaped death, he could find himself on an
operating table injected with penicillin, discovered
by Alexander Fleming of Darvel (Scotland),
and given an anaesthetic, discovered by Sir
James Young Simpson of Bathgate (Scotland).

When he came round from the anaesthetic he
would take no comfort in learning that he was
as safe as the Bank of England, founded by
William Paterson of Dumfries (Scotland).

Perhaps his only remaining hope would be to
get a transfusion of good old Scottish blood
which would give him the right him to say:

'HERE'S TAE US! WHA'S LIKE US?'

SCOTTISH HISTORY

Pre 200

82 Julius Agricola (sent in 77 to be Governor of Britain for the Roman Empire) proceeds across the River Clyde, warding off bands of pesky, warring Celts as he goes.

84 The Celtic tribes come together under Calgacus, who is then killed in a clash with the Roman army at Ardoch.

200

296 The Pictish people are first mentioned by the Romans, the name 'Pict' supposedly coming from a Latin word meaning 'painted ones'.

300

360 The Romans call the warring tribes living in Ireland the 'Scots'.

368 The Pict, Scots and Saxon tribes assault the Romans in London, burning and pillaging as they go.

500

503 The Scots leave Ireland and build a new life for themselves in Argyll.

521 St. Columba is born.

563 St. Columba, the Irish monk who converted most of Scotland to Christianity, sails from Ireland to set up a monastery on the Island of Iona. The first sighting of Nessie, the Loch Ness monster dates back to St. Columba's time. Rumour has it that after Nessie attacked a swimmer in the loch, St. Columba went into the water and ordered the beast to be gone. She obeyed.

597 St. Columba dies on the island of Iona.

600

603 St. Mungo, patron saint of Glasgow, dies. There isn't much written evidence on St. Mungo that pre-dates the 1300s but, depending on which accounts you believe, St. Mungo apparently knew St. David of Wales, as well as St. Columba. Some say he was the great-nephew of King Arthur.

685 The Angles are stopped in their advance northwards from Northumbria by the Picts at the Battle of Dunnichen.

700

704   St. Adamnan, the biographer of St. Columba, dies.

714   St. Giles, patron saint of Edinburgh (and Elgin), dies.

793   The Viking invasion of Scotland begins.

794   The Vikings attack Iona, and Orkney and Shetland become Norse colonies.

800

843   Kenneth MacAlpin (born c.800) is made the first King of the United Scots of Dalriada and the Picts. It is thought that MacAlpin's father had been beheaded whilst fighting for a Pictish king and that his mother was a Pictish princess.

858 King MacAlpin dies and is buried on the island of Iona. His brother, Donald I, becomes King of Alba, the United Kingdom of the Picts and Scots.

862 Donald I dies and his nephew Constantine I becomes king. And for the next 200 years or so there are many different kings – easy come, easy go, as you will see!

877 Aed, the son of Kenneth MacAlpin I and the brother of Constantine, becomes king but is killed within a year (see).

878 Eochaid and Giric can't agree who should be king, so they take on the job jointly and each rules his own little Pictish territory for a year or so.

889 Donald II becomes king and has Viking invasions to cope with.

900

900 Constantine II, the son of Aed, becomes king, and by all accounts a great Scottish ruler, lasting 43 years on the throne (no mean feat in this period). He has the West Saxons to contend with and suffers horrendous defeat at the Battle of Brunanburh towards the end of his rule. However, he manages to establish the Scottish church in 906, which is pretty good going, as his Pictish ancestors had suppressed this idea.

943 Malcolm I takes over as king when Constantine II goes to live in a monastery. He is killed in 954.

954 Indulf, the son of Constantine, becomes king.

962 Dubh (rather ominously, AKA The Black),

Malcolm I's son, rules.

967 Indulf's son, Cullen, becomes king.

971 Malcolm I's son, Kenneth II, rules until 995 but he can't have been that popular because he was murdered by his own subjects.

995 Constantine III has a brief two-year reign as King of the Scots before being killed (rumour has it by Kenneth III, who succeeded him. Now there's a motive!).

997 So now Kenneth III, son of Dubh, becomes king but is himself killed later on by none other than … Malcolm II, of course!

1000

1005 Malcolm II has just killed Kenneth III to become

king. He actually has a fairly long reign – until 1034 – and rules over what is more or less Scotland, land mass wise, as it is today.

1018 Whilst the English are preoccupied with Viking raids, Malcolm II advances south and wins the Battle of Carham, restoring Lothian to Scotland.

1034 Duncan I becomes King of Scotland, but he has his dreaded cousin Macbeth to deal with. Actually, to be fair here, Macbeth probably has a more rightful claim to the throne than Duncan.

1040 So Macbeth kills Duncan I in battle and becomes king, inspiring Shakespeare to write about him in time to come. He reigns during a period of relative peace and wealth.

1057 Malcolm III catches up with Macbeth in battle and in turn kills him. Macbeth is buried on the island of Iona.

Lulach, Macbeth's stepson, becomes king and is crowned at Scone. Apparently he was nicknamed The Simple. Needless to say, he doesn't survive long.

1058 Malcolm III, desperate to become king now, kills King Lulach at Essie in Strathbogie and takes the throne, founding the Canmore dynasty and being the last of the Celtic kings.

1059 No kings are killed but a weasel, just to ease the monotony, bites King Malcolm. Serves him right.

1070 Malcolm III marries again, this time a Saxon princess called Margaret.

1093 Malcolm III is killed at the Battle of Alnwick, alongside his eldest son by Margaret. Margaret, it is said, dies broken-hearted as a result and is buried in the church founded by her in Dunfermline. She is later to become St. Margaret. Meanwhile, Malcolm III is succeeded by his brother Donald III, AKA The Bane (Fair) who is 60.

1094 Donald III is deposed by his own nephew, Duncan II. But Duncan is killed later this year, so Donald regains the throne.

1097 Malcolm III's son, Edgar, invades Scotland and Donald is defeated and deposed again.

1100

1107 Edgar dies and as a result Scotland is disunited. Alexander I becomes King of Scots, and, not to be outdone, his brother David I becomes King in Lothian and Strathclyde.

1124 Unity is restored when Alexander I dies and David I becomes King of Scots. His reign is one of the most important in Scotland's history and he achieves a lot for Scotland, extending Scottish borders to the River Tees, including all of Northumberland.

1138 David I is defeated by the English at the Battle of the Standard in Yorkshire.

1139 King Stephen of England recognizes David I as king of an independent Scotland, with the Second Treaty of Durham (9 April).

1141 Malcolm IV is born.

1153 David I dies in Carlisle.

Malcolm IV is crowned King of Scotland at Scone, aged only 11. He ends up with the nickname The Maiden – for being unmarried and dying without an heir.

1165 Malcolm IV dies at Jedburgh Castle, and is succeeded by his brother William I (AKA The Lion), who is crowned at Scone.

1173 King William I invades England.

1174 William I is surprised and seized by the English at Alnwick. Henry sends him to Normandy where he is imprisoned in the castle of Falaise until the following December. (William plea-bargains with Henry and is released after promising to give up to Henry five of his main fortresses.)

1178 William founds Arbroath Abbey.

1181 The Pope excommunicates William I and lays the kingdom under an interdict.

1198 William's son, Alexander II, is born.

1200

1200 William pays homage to King John at Lincoln for the lands that he held in England.

1214 William I dies at Stirling Castle and is buried in the Abbey of Arbroath, which he had founded in 1178, in honour of Thomas a Becket. The monastery has by this time become one of the richest of its kind in Scotland. William is succeeded by his son, Alexander II.

King Alexander II is crowned at Scone, at the age of 16. He goes on to earn a reputation for being a wise and just ruler and manages to maintain peace with England – no easy task.

1218 Pope Honorius III affirms the independence of the Scottish Church.

1221 King Alexander II marries Henry III's sister, Joan.

1241 Alexander III is born at Roxburgh.

1249 King Alexander II dies on the Isle of Kerrara, Oban Bay. Alexander III is crowned at Scone, aged only eight. He is later to marry Henry III's daughter, Margaret.

1263 King Haakon of Norway invades Scotland, but the Scots are victorious, and the rest of Alexander III's reign is fairly peaceful. Haakon dies towards the very end of the year in Orkney.

1266 The Treaty of Perth is signed, whereby Norway renounces her claim to the Hebrides and the Isle of Man.

1271 The Bruces, already a powerful and rich family, and now linked to Scottish royalty through marriage, acquire the Earldom of Carrick.

1274 Of Norman and Celtic ancestry, Robert the Bruce is born on 11 July. It is generally believed that he was born at Turnberry Castle, Ayreshire, although some accounts point to other possible birthplaces, in particular Lochmaben Castle in Annandale, Dumfriesshire which was the seat of the Bruce family, but which is now a ruin.

1285 Alexander III marries for the second time.

1286 Alexander III accidentally falls from his horse to his death in Fife, apparently trying to get to see his new wife.

Guardians are elected to govern Scotland.

The Bruces assert their claim to the throne.

It is decided that Margaret, Maid of Norway ('Eiriksdotter' – daughter of King Erik II), should ascend the throne.

1290 Queen Margaret dies en route from Norway to Scotland.

Despite Scottish resistance, King Edward I of England proclaims himself Overlord of Scotland.

John Balliol lays claim to the crown, a claim disputed by several competitors, the most famous of whom being Robert the Bruce.

1291 Claimants to the Scottish throne meet King Edward I at Norham on Tweed to resolve the succession. Edward I decides in Balliol's favour, against The Bruce (AKA The Competitor).

1292 John Balliol (later AKA Turncoat or Empty Coat) is crowned King of Scotland. He accepts King Edward I of England as his feudal superior.

1295 The signing of the Auld Alliance between King John Balliol of Scotland and King Philippe IV of France promises mutual help against the English and is one of the world's oldest mutual defense treaties – pas mal, eh?

1296 King Edward I takes Berwick-Upon-Tweed and

then defeats the Scots at the Battle of Dunbar.

King John Ballist abdicates in Mantrose.

England gains control of Scotland and King Edward I takes Scotland's Coronation Stone – the Stone of Destiny or Stone of Scone – to London's Westminster Abbey. (Later, in 1950, the stone is taken by student Scottish nationalists and returned to Scotland. In 1996 it becomes officially ensconced in Edinburgh Castle.)

To add insult to injury, King Edward I, at a parliament at Berwick-upon-Tweed, forces Scottish landowners to swear allegiance to him – or forfeit their lands.

1297 The Battle of Stirling Bridge takes place. William Wallace (later to be famously portrayed by Mel Gibson in the film Braveheart and thus made known to many young Scots who'd previously never heard of him) defeats an English army led by the Earl of Surrey.

Although vastly outnumbered, Wallace and his men cleverly force the English to cross Stirling Bridge and promptly slaughter them as they do so. Wallace has an overwhelming victory and some 5,000 Englishmen die. Never before has a Scottish army so triumphed over the English. Wallace captures Stirling Castle and Scotland is nearly free.

1298 Wallace is duly knighted and appointed Guardian of Scotland.

Alas, victory is short-lived as there is defeat for the Scots under Wallace at the Battle of Falkirk, where King Edward I's army uses longbows for the first time. As many as 10,000 Scots die, Wallace's reputation as a military leader is ruined and he is forced to go into hiding.

Bruce and Comyn are appointed guardians when Wallace leaves the post empty.

1299 Regency is appointed; with The Bruce and his

rival Comyn being at the head of it. Bruce keeps up the appearance of loyalty to Edward for several years to come.

The Scots take Stirling Castle.

1300

1302 The Bruce submits to Edward I and marries Elizabeth de Burgh. (Not the lady in red.)

1303 The Scots army (comprising 8,000 men), led by Sir Simon Fraser, Sinclair of Rosslyn and Red Comyn, surprise the English army (made up of a staggering 30,000 men) and defeat them at the Battle of Roslin.

France and England make a peace treaty, not only excluding the Scots but also releasing forces to attack Scotland. Merde!

1304 Edward I captures the last of the Scottish castles – Stirling.

John Comyn submits to Edward I.

Robert the Bruce's father, the Earl of Carrick, dies and Robert finds himself in competition for the throne with the equally determined Balliol / Comyn family.

1305 William Wallace is betrayed by Ralph Rae and captured by the English near Glasgow. He is condemned as a traitor to the king even though, as he correctly maintains, he has never once sworn allegiance to Edward.

On 23rd August 1305 he is executed. Wallace's fate is in line with the custom of the time: a cruel and painful traitor's end. He is dragged to the place of execution, hanged by the neck until semi-conscious, and then disembowelled whilst still alive. His internal organs are burned before his eyes before he is decapitated and his body quartered. His head is impaled on a spike and displayed at London Bridge, his right arm on the bridge at Newcastle-upon-Tyne, his left arm at Berwick, his right leg at Perth, and left leg at Aberdeen. Edward probably thinks that at last – by capturing and executing Wallace – he has broken the spirit of the Scots. How wrong can you get? By executing Wallace so brutally, all Edward succeeds in doing is to make a martyr of a popular Scottish military leader and in so doing fire the Scottish people's determination to be free. (In the 1860s a monument to Wallace is built at Abbey Craig, near Stirling – overlooking the location of the glorious Battle of Stirling Bridge.)

1306 Robert the Bruce kills Red Comyn during a heated argument at Greyfriars, a Franciscan church in Dumfries. Worse, Red's uncle, Sir Robert Comyn is killed by Bruce's followers when he rushes to defend his nephew. A big problem for The Bruce now: not only is he responsible for the death of a well-respected noble, but he has also killed him in a place of holy worship. Pope Clement V excommunicates him from the Church. Despite all this, he is crowned King Robert I (The Bruce) at Scone by Isobel of Buchan. But he is outlawed by Edward I and hunted by Aymer de Valence, the brother-in-law of Comyn. The Bruce's army is routed at Methven. He attacks and defeats John MacDougall of Lorne, kinsman of John Comyn, at the Battle of Dalry. But reprisals abound. Despite Bruce sending his family to Kildrummy Castle in Aberdeenshire for safety, his wife and daughter are imprisoned, his brother Nigel is taken and executed and his sister Mary and Countess Isabella are put in cages.

1307 The Scots at the Battle of Loudon Hill, near Darvel, crush the English forces.

King Edward I of England dies at Burgh on Sands.

Robert the Bruce defeats John Comyn's troops at the Battle of Inverurie.

1308 The scholar and philosopher, John Duns Scotus, dies. His dry subtleties lead to the word 'duns' or 'dunce' meaning dull and incapable of learning. (He is later beatified by Pope John Paul II in 1993.)

1309 King Robert the Bruce convenes his first parliament, at St. Andrews.

1310 Edward II invades Scotland.

1311 The Bruce gets his own back and attacks northern England.

1312 Robert the Bruce signs the Treaty of Inverness, with Norway, where his sister Isabel is Queen. This fixes good relations between the two countries.

1313 The Bruce captures Dumfries and Perth and conquers southwest Scotland again.

He also invades Isle of Man.

1314 A great year for the Scots: James Douglas captures Roxburgh Castle, Thomas Randolph captures Edinburgh Castle and The Bruce thrashes and humiliates Edward II at the Battle of Bannockburn. The English leave Scotland to her independence.

1315 An Act of Succession makes Edward Bruce the heir presumptive.

1316 Robert II, the first of the Stuart line, and the only son of Walter Stuart and Marjory (daughter of Robert the Bruce) is born. But Marjorie Bruce dies giving birth to him.

1318 The Bruce captures Berwick on Tweed.

Edward Bruce is killed and so the succession is settled on the young Robert.

A two-year truce is declared.

1320 The Declaration of Arbroath is written to get

the Pope to recognize Scottish independence from England. 'For we fight not for glory nor for riches nor for honour, but only and alone for freedom, which no good man surrenders but with his life.' The Pope accepts the Declaration. [*See full text of the Declaration on page 146.*]

1322 Edward II invades Scotland for the last time. And The Bruce raids England, defeating Edward II at the Battle of Old Byland.

1324 David II is born.

The Pope recognizes The Bruce as King of Scotland.

1326 The Bruce renews the Auld Alliance between France and Scotland, with the Treaty of Corbeil.

1327 Edward II of England is deposed.

Edward III advances on Scotland.

The Scots invade northern England, with James

Douglas and Thomas Randolph defeating the English at Stanhope Park.

1328 Scotland's independence is recognized by the Treaty of Edinburgh – Northampton, between Robert I and Edward III, and so ends the 30 years of Wars of Independence.

David Bruce marries Edward III's sister Joan.

1329 A few months after Scotland's independence from England, The Bruce dies at Cardross Castle and is succeeded by his son, David II. The Bruce may well have died of leprosy.

1330 James Douglas dies in Spain, trying to take The Bruce's heart to the crusades – it is now buried in Melrose Abbey.

1332 Edward Balliol, son of John Balliol, defeats the Regent, Earl of Mar, at the Battle of Dupplin near Perth.

Edward Balliol is crowned at Scone. He formally

acknowledges King Edward III of England as his feudal superior.

Balliol is deposed by supporters of David II in December 1332, restored in 1333, deposed again in 1334, restored in 1335 and finally deposed in 1341. Enough deposing and restoring to confuse anyone!

1333 King Edward III orders the capture of the Isle of Man from the Scots.

Balliol and Edward III route Sir Archibald Douglas (guardian of David II) at the Battle of Halidon Hill, where the Scots face heavy losses.

1337 Robert III is born at Scone.

1341 Edinburgh Castle is captured from the English.

1346 Acting on pleas from the French (whom England had beaten at the Battle of Crécy), King David

II attacks England with a view to capturing Durham. The Battle of Neville's Cross takes place, after which David II is seized by the English King Edward III, taken to the Tower and imprisoned.

1357 The English, as a result of the Treaty of Berwick, free David II from imprisonment.

1371 David II dies and his nephew, King Robert II (AKA Robert The Steward or Robert Stewart), is crowned at Scone, at the grand old age of 55. He is the first Stewart sovereign in Scotland.

The Treaty of Vincennes creates a fresh Franco-Scottish alliance.

1373 King Robert II holds Parliament at Scone. It is resolved that his son, the Earl of Carrick, should succeed him as king (and be called Robert III, although his son was actually baptised John).

1384 Edward III's son, John of Gaunt, attacks Scotland.

1390 Robert II dies at Dundonald Castle and is buried at Scone.

King Robert III (actual name John, not Robert), eldest son of Robert II, is crowned at Scone, aged about 50. He has the reputation of being a bit weak and by all accounts he leaves the main power in the hands of his brother, the Duke of Albany (previously the Earl of Fife).

The Form of Cury (which means cookery) is written by one of King Richard II's cooks. It is the first known English cookery book and contains a recipe for – you guessed it! – haggis.

1394 James I, the future King of Scots, son of Robert III, is born.

1400

1400 War breaks out with England.

1402 The Earl of Douglas has marched through Durham and sacked the town, but then has to confront Sir Henry Percy's forces at the Battle of Homildon Hill. The Scots are great in number but are attacked with arrows, suffer heavy losses and Douglas is seized.

1405 Robert III sends his son James to France for safety, but James is captured by the English near Flamborough Head and kept prisoner for 18 years.

1406 King Robert III dies and James I becomes king (but has a long wait to be crowned, as he is a prisoner of the English until 1423).

1411 Donald, Lord of the Isles, fights an indecisive but gory battle against the Earl of Mar at the Battle of Harlow. At the time, both sides thought they had lost and yet their descendants both thought they had won! A great thing, hindsight…

1412 The University of St. Andrews is founded – before the golf course was considered. Priorities wrong even then!

1421 Scottish and French troops, under the command of the Earl of Buchan, defeat the English forces at Baugé in Anjou.

1423 The Treaty of London brings about the release of James I – who by this time has been in captivity in England since 1405. Once released, he loses no time in punishing those who had not taken steps to get him out of prison and who had governed in his absence.

1424 King James I is crowned at Scone.

James I marries Lady Jane Beaufort, daughter of the Earl of Somerset.

The parliament convened by James I approves

the arrest of a number of the Scottish nobility.

1430 James II is born.

1437 James I is murdered in his bed in his apartment in Perth by enemies – a group of conspirators led by Sir Robert Graham.

James II is crowned King at Kelso Abbey, rather than at the traditional Scone.

1448 The Scots, led by Hugh Douglas, the Earl of Ormonde, drive back the invading English near Gretna, at the Battle of Sark.

The Franco-Scottish alliance is renewed at Tours.

1451 The University of Glasgow is founded at the request of James II.

James III is born in Stirling.

1452 James II kills William Douglas in Stirling.

1457 James II decrees in an Act of Parliament that

there should be regular target practice and military parades and that 'football and golf be not be allowed'. This is the first time that the games are mentioned in Scottish documents.

1460 King James II is killed rather gruesomely by an exploding canon during the siege of Roxburgh Castle.

James III is crowned King at Kelso Abbey.

1472 Orkney and Shetland are annexed from Norway.

1473 James IV is born.

1482 Berwick-upon-Tweed finally cedes to England after changing hands no fewer than twelve times!

1488 King James III dies, having earned the reputation of being rather weak, and as a result never gaining the respect of the Scottish nobility.

The 15-year-old James IV is crowned king at

Scone. (He was to reign until 1513, falling with the finest of Scotland's nobility at the disastrous Battle of Flodden.)

1494 The University of Aberdeen is founded.

1495 Pope Alexander VI issues a bull confirming the foundation of Aberdeen University.

1500

1502 King Henry VII of England gives his daughter, Margaret Tudor, in marriage to James IV of Scotland.

1503 King James IV marries Margaret Tudor. The marriage is known as the Union of the Thistle and the Rose. Pope Alexander VI issues a bull confirming the marriage and the

Treaty of Everlasting Peace between Scotland and England.

1512 James V is born.

Under the terms of a treaty with France (the Auld Alliance), all Scottish citizens become French and vice versa – the first attempt at a European Union.

1513 James IV is killed in the ruinous (and some say avoidable) Battle of Flodden, Northumberland. The head count is fairly equal for both sides but the English have far superior fighting equipment to the Scots. Losses on both sides are heavy, but the Scots take the brunt of it, with somewhere between 5,000 and 10,000 dying, including many noblemen.

James V succeeds, despite being only 18 months old, and is crowned at Stirling Castle.

1522 England declares war on both Scotland and France.

1526 Sir Walter Scott of Buccleuch tries to rescue King James V from the hands of Douglas, the Earl of Angus, at the Battle of Melrose.

1528 Patrick Hamilton, a Protestant martyr, is charged with heresy and burned at the stake in St. Andrews.

1532 King James V establishes paid judges to sit at the Court of Session, the highest civil court in Scotland.

1538 James V marries Marie de Guise, a French noblewoman.

1542 Mary, Queen of Scots, is born at Linlithgow Palace.

Henry VIII attacks Scotland and his forces easily overcome James V's army. James V dies at Falkland Palace, apparently after suffering a mental breakdown. He leaves his crown to his daughter Mary Stuart, who is only eight days old at the time! She is

James V's only legitimate child.

1543 Henry VIII and the Earl of Arron (Regent of Scotland) sign the Treaty of Greenwich, agreeing the betrothal of Mary, Queen of Scots, (aged six months) and Edward Prince of Wales (aged six years).

Mary, Queen of Scots, is crowned at Stirling Castle.

1544 Fierce, bloody fighting (the Battle of Blar-Nan-Leine) takes place between the Clan Fraser and the Clans Ranald, Cameron and Donald. The outcome is terrible, with only four of the 300-strong Fraser Clan surviving and nearly 800 men dying in total.

1545 Scottish forces led by the Earl of Douglas defeat an English army twice their size at the Battle of Ancrum Morr.

Andrew Melville, the 'true father of Presbyterianism in Scotland', is born.

1546 George Wishart, a 33-year-old Protestant martyr, is betrayed to Cardinal Beaton, imprisoned for heresy and then burned at the stake just outside St. Andrews Castle. A short while after his death, some of his friends murder Cardinal Beaton in revenge. Wishart was a confidant and mentor of John Knox.

Henry Stuart, the dashing Lord Darnley, is born.

1547 The English defeat the Scots at the Battle of Pinkie Cleugh, near Edinburgh. The battle, triggered by the English demands that Edward VI of England (aged 10) should marry Mary, Queen of Scots, (aged five) is an event known as the Rough Wooing. Something like 15,000 Scots were killed and 1,500 captured, whilst the English losses amounted to barely 500.

1548 The Treaty of Haddington, between France and Scotland, confirms the betrothal of Mary, Queen of Scots, and the Dauphin of France, François Valois.

1558 Mary, Queen of Scots, marries the French Dauphin (who is 14) at Notre Dame in Paris.

Walter Mylne, the last pre-Reformation martyr, is charged with heresy and burned to death at the stake in St. Andrews.

1559 Ordained in St. Giles Cathedral, Edinburgh, John Knox becomes the first Protestant minister appointed in the city. His sermon in Perth begins the Reformation in Scotland.

King Henri of France dies and François becomes king.

1560 The second Treaty of Berwick between England and Scotland provides English assistance to get rid of Mary de Guise's French forces from Scotland.

The Treaty of Edinburgh between France and England recognises the sovereignty of Mary, Queen of Scots, and her first husband François II.

Latin Mass is prohibited in Scotland by Parliament as Protestant faith gains the upper hand.

The first General Assembly of the Church of Scotland is held.

1561 Mary, Queen of Scots, lands at Leith on her return from France, after the death of her husband, King François II.

1565 Mary, Queen of Scots, meets Lord Darnley for the first time. There is instant attraction and they marry the same year.

1566 Mary, Queen of Scots, gives birth to the future King James VI of Scotland and I of England.

1567 Lord Darnley, Mary's husband, is murdered.

Mary marries the Earl of Bothwell.

Mary spends her last night in Edinburgh, at the house of Sir Simon Preston, the Lord Provost, on the Royal Mile, prior to her imprisonment at Loch Leven Castle two days later.

Mary abdicates (24 July) and five days later James VI, aged just 13 months, is crowned at the Church of the Holy Rude, beside Stirling Castle. James Stewart, the Earl of Moray and a half-brother of Mary, Queen of Scots, is proclaimed Regent of Scotland.

1568 Mary, Queen of Scots, escapes from Loch Leven Castle in May. Less than two weeks later as she is trying to make her way to shelter at Dumbarton Castle, she is defeated at the Battle of Langside. She flees, eventually sailing from Port Mary across the Solway Firth to exile in England. Out of the frying pan and in to the fire!

1570 James Stewart is murdered in Linlithgow, triggering civil war.

The Earl of Lennox is appointed Regent of Scotland.

1571 The Earl of Lennox is murdered. The Earl of Mar is appointed Regent (but dies in October 1572).

1572 John Knox, the leading reformer of Church of Scotland, dies.

1573 Sir William Kirkcaldy of Grange is executed, after defending Edinburgh Castle on behalf of Mary, Queen of Scots (May 1568 – May 1573).

1581 James Douglas, the 4th Earl of Morton, is beheaded in Edinburgh Grassmarket for the murder of Lord Darnley.

1582 The University of Edinburgh is founded.

James VI (aged nearly eight) is abducted and taken to the Castle of Ruthven by the Earls of Mar and Gowrie – this is the so-called Ruthven Raid.

1583 James VI escapes from Ruthven Castle.

1585 The poet William Drummond is born.

1586 Mary, Queen of Scots, recognises Philip II of Spain as her heir.

1587 Mary, Queen of Scots, is beheaded at Fotheringay Castle on the orders of Elizabeth I. By all accounts, Mary is said to have pardoned her executioners with the words, 'I forgive you with all my heart, for now, I hope, you shall make an end of all my troubles.'

1592 The Earl of Moray is murdered in Donibristle.

1600

1600 King Charles I is born in Dunfermline.

Scotland celebrates New Year for the first time on 1 January (previously the start of the year had been regarded as 25 March). England carries on with the old system – 25 March – until 1752. As a result, there's some contradiction between the two countries as far as the dates of historical documents are concerned from 1600 until 1752. We couldn't even agree on the date!

1603 The Battle at Glenfruin takes place – with the MacGregors slaughtering a number of Colquhouns. This is reportedly the origin of the banning of the MacGregor name.

The death of Queen Elizabeth I and the succession of King James VI brings about the Union of the Crowns of England and Scotland. James VI of Scotland becomes James I of England also – a double whammy – and is crowned as King of Great Britain and Ireland at Westminster Abbey, London.

1604 King James I authorizes a new translation

of the Bible – into English – be started.

1605 Guy Fawkes is arrested beneath the Houses of Parliament with 20 barrels of gunpowder to blow up parliament and the king. Parliament declares the 5th of November a day of public thanksgiving.

The Union flag is adopted as the flag of England, Wales and Scotland.

1611 The King James I authorized translation of the Bible is now complete.

1615 St. John Ogilvie, a Banffshire-born Jesuit priest, is hanged for refusing to renounce the supremacy of the Pope, becoming the only Roman Catholic martyr in Scotland and canonised in 1976.

1617 John Napier, the inventor of logarithms, dies in Edinburgh.

James VI, on his only return to Scotland, puts his foot in it when he tactlessly lectures his countrymen on the 'superiority of English civilisation'.

1618 James VI imposes bishops on the Presbyterian Church of Scotland in an effort to integrate it with the Church of England. This move is really unpopular with the Scots and James becomes even more disliked, to say the least.

1624 George Heriot, goldsmith to King James VI and founder of George Heriot's School, dies.

1625 James VI dies at Theobalds Park, Hertfordshire and is buried at Westminster Abbey. His son, Charles I, becomes king.

Although born in Scotland, Charles disrespectfully shows no interest in the country and is even more disliked than his father. No mean feat.

1626 Charles I is crowned at Westminster Abbey.

1630 Charles II is born at St. James' Palace, London.

1633 King Charles I is crowned at Holyrood.

James VII is born at St. James' Palace, London.

A warrant is issued by the Privy Council to Sir John Hepburn to raise a regiment of 1,200 men to fight in the French service. The corps ultimately become the First Regiment of Foot, The Royal Scots.

1637 Charles I attempts to further anglicize the Church of Scotland by introducing a new prayer book, setting off riots at St. Giles Cathedral in Edinburgh. Feisty Jenny Geddes throws a stool in St. Giles in protest.

1638 As Charles I regards protests against the prayer book as treason, he forces the Scots to choose between their church and the king. A Covenant swearing to resist these changes to the death is signed in Greyfriars Church in Edinburgh. Hundreds, if not thousands, of Scots, accept the Covenant.

1639 Charles I calls a General Assembly, effectively abolishing the unpopular Scottish bishops. An agreement is reached through the Treaty of Berwick.

1640 Charles I's peace collapses and the Scots show force by marching on Newcastle.

1641 Having no realistic chance of opposing the Scots, Charles I sees sense and negotiates a truce at Ripon.

1642 Civil war breaks out in England. The Scottish Covenanters side with the English rebels who take power. Civil strife spills into Scotland as the Earl of Montrose sides with King Charles.

The Scots Guards regiment is formed.

1644 A Scottish army under the Earl of Leven crosses the river Tweed into England. It remains in England for three years, playing an important part in the civil war.

Scots forces under David Leslie help in the victory of the Parliamentary forces over the Royalists at the Battle of Marston Moor.

The Battle of Aberdeen takes place, with James Graham, the 1st Marquess of Montrose, sacking the city.

1646 King Charles I surrenders to Lord Leven.

1647 Charles I, imprisoned at Carisbrooke Castle, reaches an agreement with the Scots who offer military aid in exchange for a promise to establish Presbyterianism in England (but only for three years).

1649 Charles I is executed at Whitehall, despite protests from the Scots. Throughout his trial and right up to his death he apparently maintains his dignity and shows great courage.

Charles, the Duke of Rothesay, is proclaimed King Charles II of Scots in Edinburgh – but not in England. The English Parliament declares

England a republic.

Oliver Cromwell invades Scotland.

1650 General George Monck commands a regiment under Oliver Cromwell in Scotland.

Montrose loses his last fight – the Battle of Carbisdale. After going on the run he is betrayed, seized and sent to Edinburgh where a death sentence awaits him. He is executed at Mercat Cross, Edinburgh, his head fixed on a spike at the Tolbooth and his arms and legs nailed to the gates of Glasgow, Aberdeen, Perth and Stirling as a warning to look both ways before crossing the road. (After the Restoration in 1660, Montose's embalmed heart and bones are buried at St. Giles Cathedral, Edinburgh.)

1651 Charles II is crowned King of Scots at Scone – the last coronation of a king on Scottish soil.

General Monck, now Commander-in-Chief in Scotland, continues the war against the Royalist and Covenanters. He captures Stirling, Dundee and Aberdeen.

1652 James Granger, the minister at Kinneff, Aberdeenshire, saves the Scottish Royal Regalia (crown, sceptre and sword) from the invading army of Oliver Cromwell, after they had been smuggled from Dunnottar Castle, which was under siege.

1653 Scotland is declared a republic. The English MP, Oliver Cromwell, becomes Lord Protector of England, Scotland and Ireland.

1658 Oliver Cromwell dies.

1659 A frisky camel causes a sensation in Edinburgh. (They didn't have much entertainment in those days, with all that fighting going on!)

1660 Charles II returns to England on 29 May – now known as Royal Oak Day.

1661 The first newspaper in Scotland is published.

Mercurius Caledonius offers coverage of 'the affairs now in agitation in Scotland, with a survey of foreign intelligence.' It ceases publication after only nine issues.

Charles II is crowned at Westminster Abbey.

Many Scottish historical records are lost when the ship Elizabeth of Burntisland sinks off the English coast. (The records had been taken to London by Oliver Cromwell and were being returned to Edinburgh.)

1665 Queen Anne, the last of the Stewart monarchs, is born.

1671 Rob Roy MacGregor, the famous cattle thief, general troublemaker and Jacobite rebel, is born. He owes his nickname Ruadh or Roy to his wild red hair.

1673 King James VII marries Mary of Modena.

1678 The Earl of Mar is commissioned to

raise a regiment – nicknamed the Earl of Mar's Gray Breeks – that becomes the Royal Scots Fusiliers.

1681 The poet and bookseller Allan Ramsay is born. He went on to found the first travelling library in the UK.

1682 The National Library of Scotland – now one of the UK's four copyright deposit libraries – is founded.

1685 King Charles II, AKA 'the merry monarch', dies. His last words to his brother James are apparently, 'Don't let poor Nellie starve,' a reference to his favourite mistress, Nell Gwynne.

James VII is crowned at Westminster Abbey.

1688 James Francis Stuart is born. In honour of the Old Pretender, this is known as White Rose Day in Jacobite circles.

William of Orange lands in Southwest England.

At the end of the year, King James VII is deposed by his nephew and son-in-law, William of Orange, and flees, dropping the Great Seal into the murky river Thames.

1689 William of Orange and Mary II become joint sovereigns of the UK.

The Earl of Leven raises a Border regiment to protect Edinburgh against the Jacobites. It later becomes the King's Own Scottish Borderers.

Scottish Parliament declares that James VII has forfeited the Scottish throne.

The Battle of Killiecrankie takes place, with Viscount Dundee (John Graham of Claverhouse) leading a force of Jacobite Highlanders to overcome the forces of King William, led by General Hugh Mackay. Viscount Dundee is killed leading the charge.

The Earl of Angus forms the Cameronians into a regiment (so named after the Covenanter Richard Cameron).

1690 The Scots Parliament sanctions the establishment of a Presbyterian religious system, rejecting Episcopacy.

William III defeats James VII in the Battle of the Boyne, Ireland.

1692 The massacre of Glencoe occurs. Clan Campbell sides with the king and murders members of the McDonald clan.

1694 Mary II dies and her husband, William of Orange, continues to reign on his own.

The MacGregor name is outlawed. Rob Roy takes his mother's maiden name of Campbell.

1695 The Darien Company forms to set up a Scottish colony in Panama.

The Scottish Parliament establishes a

General Post Office.

The Bank of Scotland is founded (still operating to this day).

1698 The Darien Expedition lands in Panama.

1700

1700 The Scottish settlement in Darien, Panama, is abandoned after two years of fever and death. Much of Scotland is ruined and this fact leads to the union with England seven years later.

1701 The Scottish-born pirate 'Captain' William Kidd is tried for piracy at London's Old Bailey, found guilty and hanged on 23 May.

The deposed King James VII dies at Château de Saint Germain-en-Laye, near Paris.

1702   King William III dies and Queen Anne (the daughter of King James VII) succeeds him at the ripe old age of 37.

1704   The Scottish Parliament passes the Act of Security. This allows Scotland to choose a successor to Queen Anne, other than the one elected by the English Parliament, if Scottish conditions are not met. This precipitates the demands in London for an Act of Union of the two parliaments.

Andrew Selkirk, a young Scottish sailor, is marooned on the Pacific Island of Juan Fernández (over 400 miles off the coast of Chile) for four years, inspiring one of the most famous novels in the English language: Robinson Crusoe.

1706   The last Scottish Parliament meets in Edinburgh before the Union with Westminster.

1707   The Treaty (or Act) of Union is passed; Scotland

formally unites with England to form Great Britain. The Scottish Parliament basically votes itself out of existence and is formally dissolved. The Earl of Seafield, James Ogilvy, apparently says, 'There's an end to an auld sang.'

The parliament sits for the last time and will not do so again till 1999.

1711 Rob Roy borrows a substantial amount of money from the Duke of Montrose, but one of his trusted friends disappears with it. A warrant is then issued for Rob Roy's arrest; he loses his lands and becomes an outlaw.

David Hume, the philosopher and historian, is born. In his Essays: Moral, Political and Literary, The Stoic, 1742, he says, 'The great end of all human industry is the attainment of happiness. For this were arts invented, science cultivated, laws ordained and societies modelled by the most profound wisdom of patriots and legislators.'

1713 The artist Allan Ramsay is born.

1714 Queen Anne dies and George I, Elector of Hanover, becomes king. He speaks only German, knows little about Scotland and cares not a jot to learn.

1715 The Earl of Mar unfurls the standard of the Old Pretender at the start of the Jacobite Uprising.

The Battle of Sheriffmuir takes place and a force of Jacobites led by the Earl of Mar, fights an inconclusive battle against a Hanoverian force led by the Duke of Argyll.

Rob Roy misses this battle because of mixed allegiances (Jacobite sympathies v. the interests of his benefactor, the Duke of Argyll). Nevertheless, he is charged with treason.

1719 The marriage ceremony of Prince James Francis Edward Stewart (the Old Pretender) and Princess Maria Clementina Sobieska takes place. The

Polish Princess had been kidnapped on her way to the original wedding, escaped and married James by proxy earlier in the year.

Daniel Defoe's Robinson Crusoe is published, inspired by Alexander Selkirk's four-year stay on an uninhabited island.

1720 Charles Edward Stewart, AKA Bonnie Prince Charlie, is born in Rome. He is known as the Young Pretender and is the grandson of James VII of Scotland.

1723 Adam Smith, the economist and philosopher, is born. He becomes famous as the author of An Inquiry into the Nature and Causes of the Wealth of Nations.

1725 In this year the Black Watch regiment is commissioned under General Wade to patrol the Highlands. General Wade... General Wade... This is the man referred to in the 6th verse of God Save the Queen [see p.155] – as the one with the ability to crush and tame those rebellious Scots… He was Commander in Chief of 'North Britain' at this time (until 1740). To give him his due, he did improve the military routes across the Highlands by having many roads and bridges built.

Rob Roy also turns himself in to General Wade (not literally!) this year and is issued a pardon by the king.

1727 King George I dies and George II becomes king.

1728 The Royal Bank invents the first overdraft (for which we are ever thankful).

Robert Adam is born. (He later becomes a leading architect of his age, noted for many elegant terraces in Edinburgh and London.)

James Cook, the famous explorer of the seas, is born to Scottish parents in Yorkshire.

1729 Two women are arrested in Edinburgh for

wearing men's clothing…

John Law, the financier and founder of New Orleans, dies.

1734 Rob Roy MacGregor dies. Having been hunted for some ten years on high treason charges when he eventually surrendered (in 1725), he was permitted to end his days at Balquhidder, where he is buried.

1736 James Watt, the inventor and engineer, is born. He leads a talented life as a mathematical instrument maker, develops the steam engine, and invents the condenser and copying machine.

1740 James Boswell, the biographer of Dr. Johnson, is born at Blair's Land, Parliament Square, Edinburgh.

1744 The world's first golf club – the Honourable Company of Edinburgh Golfers – is founded.

Patrick Ferguson, the inventor of the breech-loading rifle, is born.

1745 The French-backed Jacobite rebellion begins, intending to restore the Stewarts to the throne of Britain.

Prince Charlie proclaims his father as King James VIII of Scotland at Perth. He then occupies Edinburgh and takes up residence at Holyrood Palace.

The Scots see victory at the Battle of Prestonpans. The Jacobite army of just over 3,000 under Bonnie Prince Charlie heavily defeat the English Royal forces led by Sir John Cope.

The Jacobite Scottish army advances as far south as Derby but then head back north disappointed that more English Jacobites did not support and join them.

1746 The Rebellion ends in bloody failure at Culloden, where the Duke of Cumberland defeats Bonnie Prince Charlie.

Actually, more Scots fought on the government's side than on the Jacobites' at Culloden.

After an all night march the exhausted Highlanders are no match for the well-disciplined Government forces. They are thoroughly beaten and no mercy is shown to the wounded and the fleeing. For months after this crofts are burned and Jacobites hunted down and put to the sword.

Flora MacDonald meets the Bonnie Prince and persuades him to wear women's clothes as part of the escape plan from the Outer Hebrides to Skye. He escapes capture by sailing to France aboard the French ship 'L'Heureux'.

The wearing of the kilt is banned.

1747 Lord Lovat is executed at Tower Hill for high treason – the last person in Britain to be beheaded.

James Lind begins a controlled experiment that demonstrates that citrus fruits can prevent scurvy, a disease contracted by sailors on long voyages. (The lime juice which eventually becomes standard issue to British sailors is behind the term 'limey' as a name for British overseas.)

1750 Sir William Fettes, the merchant who made his fortune from tea and wine, is born. He later leaves money to found Fettes College (built in 1870).

1752 Colin Campbell of Glenure, known as the Red Fox, and a notorious persecutor of Jacobites after Culloden, is shot in Aping. Alan Breck (later made famous in Robert Louis Stevenson's Kidnapped and Catriona) is accused (though no evidence is put forward) and flees to France. James Stewart (a friend of Red Fox) is arrested and found guilty, despite a lack of evidence, by a jury in Inveraray, presided over by the Duke of Argyll.

With the adoption of the Gregorian calendar, 3 September 1752 becomes 14 of September. Crowds gather in the streets demanding, 'Give us back our 11 days.'

1754 The St. Andrews Society of Golfers is constituted. (In 1834 it becomes the Royal and Ancient Golf Club.)

1756 Sir Henry Raeburn, famous for painting the portraits of many of the citizens of Edinburgh, is born.

1758 James Taylor, who developed the steamboat, is born.

1759 Robert Burns – one of the most famous of all Scots! – is born. He is responsible for Auld Lang Syne [see p. 156], which is now sung all over the world as the New Year chimes in. Other works include Tam o'Shanter, To a Mouse, and To a Louse. Nowadays on the 25th of January the

Scots celebrate Burns' Night with much poetry, haggis and whisky!

1760 George III is crowned, beginning a 60-year reign, one of the longest in British history.

1766 James Stewart, the Old Pretender, dies.

Charles Macintosh, who patented waterproof fabric, is born. Without him we would never have had the classic joke:
'Have you got a light Mac?'
"No, but I've got a dark brown overcoat.'

1768 The first edition of the Encyclopaedia Britannica is published in Edinburgh by three people: William Smellie (editor), Colin Macfarquhar (printer) and Andrew Bell (engraver). This is a s(m)ell out and is followed in by a larger, second edition (between 1777 and 1784).

1770 The Clyde Trust is set up to convert the River Clyde (at that time a small river) into a major thoroughfare for maritime communications.

This requires a major programme of excavation and dredging.

James Bruce discovers the source of the Blue Nile – Lake Tana in northwest Ethiopia.

1771 Sir Walter Scott, the novelist, poet and great Scottish patriot (and avid collector of all things Scottish), is born. He becomes famous for his Waverley novels, Rob Roy, Ivanhoe, Marmion, and The Pirate, amongst others. It is to him that we owe the phrase, 'Oh, what a tangled web we weave, when first we practise to deceive!' (Marmion, 1808).

1772 Robert Stevenson, the distinguished builder of lighthouses, is born. He is the grandfather of Robert Louis Stevenson.

1776 Adam Smith's An Inquiry into the Nature and Causes of the Wealth of Nations is published. An excerpt: 'It is not from the benevolence of the butcher, the brewer, or the baker, that we expect our dinner, but from their regard to their own interest.'

David Hume, the philosopher and historian, dies.

1779 Lord Henry Cockburn, the noted judge, is born. In Circuit Journeys, 1847, he says, 'I never see a scene of Scotch beauty, without being thankful that I have beheld it before it has been breathed over by the angel of mechanical destruction.'

1780 The firm of James Watt and Co is established to manufacture the world's first duplicating machines.

The African explorer Alexander Laing is born.

Patrick Ferguson, inventor of the breech-loading rifle, dies.

1781 David Brewster, the inventor of the kaleidoscope, is born.

1782 James Chalmers is born in Arbroath. He is to

invent the sticky stamp and be buried with the gravestone inscription, 'Originator of the adhesive postage stamp, which saved the penny postage scheme of 1840 from collapse.'

The Highland Dress Proscription Act is repealed, allowing again the wearing of tartan and the carrying of weapons (banned as a result of the 1745 Uprising in support of Bonnie Prince Charlie).

Charles McLaren, one of the founders of The Scotsman newspaper, is born.

The Glasgow Herald newspaper is first published. It is the longest continuously published daily newspaper in Britain.

1784 The first balloon ascent in Britain takes place by James Tytler, Edinburgh.

The artist Allan Ramsay dies.

1786 The Kilmarnock Edition of the poems of Robert

Burns is first published.

1787 Built by Thomas Smith and Robert Stevenson, the first lighthouse in Scotland opens (at Kinnaird Head, Fraserburgh).

1788 Deacon William Brodie, by day a respected cabinetmaker and town councillor, is a burglar by night. After one of his gang is caught and squeals, Brodie is arrested in Amsterdam and sentenced to death by hanging. It is said that Brodie's strange behaviour inspires Robert Louis Stevenson to write The Strange Case of Dr. Jekyll and Mr Hyde.

Charles Edward Stewart, AKA Bonnie Prince Charlie, dies, allegedly despondent and an alcoholic. He is buried in St. Peter's, in Rome.

1789 The Reverend Elijah Craig is the first to produce whisky distilled from maize – trust a clergyman! He called the new liquor 'bourbon' because he lived in Bourbon County, Kentucky.

1790 Flora Macdonald, who helped save Bonnie Prince Charlie during his flight after the defeat at the Battle of Culloden, dies in Kingsburgh, Skye (in the same bed in which Charles had slept during his escape).

The economist and philosopher Adam Smith dies.

1791 James Boswell's Life of Johnson is published. An excerpt: 'We cannot tell the precise moment when friendship is formed. As in filling a vessel drop by drop, there is at last a drop that makes it run over; so in a series of kindnesses, there is at last one which makes the heart run over.'

1792 The architect Robert Adams dies.

John Paul Jones, naval hero of the American Revolution, dies; he was born in Kircudbrightshire in 1747.

1794 Robert Liston is born in Linlithgow. He later carries out the first operation in Britain with the aid of an anaesthetic.

The 4th Duke of Gordon raises The Gordon Highlanders (75th, 92nd).

The Argyllshire Highlanders, or 91st, is raised.

1795 James Boswell, the biographer of Dr. Johnson, dies.

The historian and essayist Thomas Carlyle is born. He becomes Rector of Edinburgh University in 1866 and dies in 1881. In 1838, in his Critical and Miscellaneous Essays, he declares, 'A well-written life is almost as rare as a well-spent one.'

1796 Robert Burns dies aged just 37.

The Scottish explorer Mungo Park reaches the source of the river Niger in Africa.

1799 Income tax is introduced for the first time.

1800

1802 The Edinburgh Review is first published 'to erect a higher standard of merit, and secure a bolder and purer taste in literature, and to apply philosophical principles and the maxims of truth and humanity to politics'.

1807 Henry, Cardinal of York, last of the Royal House of Stewart, dies.

1809 General Sir John Moore dies at the Battle of Corunna in Spain. A famous poem was written which begins:

'Not a drum was heard, not a funeral note,
As his corpse to the rampart we hurried;
Not a soldier discharged his farewell shot
O'er the grave where our hero we buried.'

1811 The first women's golf tournament takes place in Scotland at Musselburgh.

1813 David Livingstone, the missionary and explorer, is born in Blantyre. In the Last Journal of David Livingstone in Central Africa, 1874, he writes, 'The strangest thing I have ever seen in this country seems really to be broken-heartedness and it attacks free men who have been captured and made slaves.'

1814 Dr. John Goodsir, the Scottish anatomist, is born in Anstruther, Fife. In 1842 he shows that bacteria is the cause of disease and that it can be eliminated with selective poisons – Goodsir is here 18 years before Louis Pasteur, who is usually credited with the discovery, makes the claim. Goodsir is remembered now for his unrivalled knowledge of the anatomy of tissues and as one of the earliest and leading observers of cell-life.

Walter Scott's Waverley Novels are first published.

1815 John A. MacDonald, who becomes the first Prime Minister of the Dominion of Canada in 1867, is born at 20 Brunswick Street in Glasgow.

1819 The future Queen Victoria is born.

James Watt, the developer of steam power, dies. In a letter to his wife in 1767 he wrote, 'I think that I shall not long have anything to do with the House of Commons again – I never saw so many wrong-headed people on all sides gathered together.'

Alan Pinkerton is born in Glasgow. In 1852 he becomes the founder of the Chicago-based detective agency, which bears his name, and (from 1861 to 1862), Head of the US Secret Service.

George III dies and George IV becomes king.

1820 Sir Walter Scott is created a baronet.

1821 Tom Morris is born. He is one of golf's

founding fathers and goes on to win the British Open four times.

1822 The portrait painter Henry Raeburn dies.

1823 Charles Macintosh patents the waterproof cloth he is using to make raincoats.

1824 Edinburgh's Great Fire destroys the High Street, Parliament Square and the Tron Kirk.

The novelist and poet George MacDonald is born.

1825 The novelist R.M. Ballantyne, is born. He goes on to write 90 books, the best known being The Coral Island.

William McGonagall is born. He becomes known as Scotland's worst poet and a heroic failure! Here's what the poet Hugh McDiarmid had to say in his Scottish Eccentrics, 1936, about McGonagall's work: 'There is so much that is bad in all the poetry that Scots people know and admire that it is not surprising that for their pet example of a good bad poet they should have to go outside the range of poetry, good, bad, or indifferent altogether. McGonagall is in a very special category, and has it entirely to himself.'

1826 Robert Adamson, who collaborated with D.O. Hill to produce early portrait photography, is born.

The explorer Alexander Gordon Laing becomes the first Christian to reach Timbuctu, Africa.

Scotland's first commercial railway opens between Edinburgh and Dalkeith.

The Royal Scottish Academy, designed by the architect William Henry Playfair, opens.

Meg Dodds, the landlady of the Cleikum Inn near Peebles, produces her Cook's and Housewife's Manual, which contains two recipes for haggis. Her Inn holds gatherings for the Cleikum Club of diners who discuss national issues such as Scottish literature and customs. Sir Walter Scott is among the founders. The Club is among the first organisations to organise Burns' Night, and we all know haggis is the traditional Burns' Night dish.

1827 The foundation of the George IV Bridge, Edinburgh, is laid but the bridge is not completed until 1836 due to lack of funds.

Dr William McEwan, the brewer and philanthropist, is born.

1829 William Burke, the murderer and body snatcher of Burke and Hare fame, is executed.

The poet Alexander Smith is born. On the Writing of Essays, Dreamthorp, 1863, he says, 'It is not of so much consequence what you say, as how you say it.'

1830 King George IV dies, aged 67, and William IV ascends the throne. Supposedly Britain's fattest king, George IV liked a heartier breakfast than most, frequently devouring roast pigeons and beefsteaks, all washed down with white wine, champagne, port and brandy! If only!

1831 Scotland's first passenger railway (between Glasgow and Garnkirk) opens.

1832 The novelist and poet sir Walter Scott dies aged 61. In a letter to James Bailey, June 1817, he said, 'To live the life of an author for mere bread is perhaps the most dreadful fate that can be encountered.'

The engineer, road, bridge and canal builder Thomas Telford dies.

1835 Poet James Hogg, the Ettrick shepherd, dies (in Ettrick).

William McTaggart, the Scottish landscape painter, is born.

1836 John McAdam, the inventor of 'tar macadam' road surface, dies.

The industrialist and philanthropist Andrew Carnegie is born in Dunfermline, Fife. After emigrating to America in 1848 he becomes an iron and steel magnate and very, very rich. Unlike most rich men, he gives much of his fortune back to Scotland and America in the form of educational endowments. Even today his trustees bestow sums of his wealth to various bodies all over the world. Carnegie leaves a large sum of money to Yale University to build a golf course, and is quoted as saying, 'Golf is an indispensable adjunct to high civilization.' About his own wealth, he says, 'My chief happiness lies in the thought that even after I pass away, the wealth that came to me to administer as a sacred trust for the good of my fellowmen is to continue to benefit humanity for generations untold.'

Sir William Fettes, the merchant, dies.

1837 William IV dies and Victoria ascends the throne.

1838 Queen Victoria is crowned at Westminster Abbey.

The Clydesdale Bank is founded in Glasgow.

The 703-ton Sirius, built in Leith and carrying 90 passengers, reaches New York; the first ship to cross the Atlantic entirely under steam. A shortage of fuel results in spars and furniture being burned towards the end of the 18-day voyage. Brunel's steamship, the Great Western, arrives a day later. Not a lot of people know that!

Thomas Blake Glover, the founding father of Japan's industrialisation (including Mitsubishi) and the Japanese Navy, is born in Fraserburgh.

1840 The foundation stone for the monument to Sir Walter Scott is laid in Princes Street Gardens.

John Boyd Dunlop, the developer (not inventor) of the pneumatic tyre, is born.

1842 Queen Victoria visits Edinburgh for the first

time and opens the intercity railway between Glasgow and Edinburgh. She is to visit Scotland several times after this.

1843 Dr Henry Faulds, who established the uniqueness of fingerprints, is born in Beith, Ayrshire.

The Church of Scotland is disrupted. 474 ministers sign the Deed of Demission and form the Free Church of Scotland (AKA the Wee Free).

1846 Born in 1794, Robert Liston, now the skillful surgeon and pioneer of several new methods of amputation, performs the first operation in a British hospital using ether as an anaesthetic.

1847 Alexander Graham Bell is born in Edinburgh. He invents the telephone (patented in 1876), founds the Bell Telephone Company, invents the photophone (a prototype of fibre-optics, enabling the transmission of sound via a beam of light), as well as the metal detector (1881). He devises techniques for teaching speech to deaf people and is also credited with advancements in the aviation field. One smart cookie!

The surgeon Robert Liston dies.

1848 January 29: Greenwich Mean Time is adopted by Scotland.

Arthur James Balfour is born. He becomes Prime Minister from 1902 to 1905 and responsible for The Balfour Declaration in 1917 promising the Zionists a home in Palestine. He dies in 1930.

1849 Queen Victoria visits Glasgow and is the first monarch to visit the city since James VI in the 16th century. Having visited the 'second city of the Empire' she is reputed to have said that she did not wish to repeat the experience...

1850 Sir Thomas Lipton, founder of the Lipton's grocery chain and a millionaire by the age of 30, is born in Glasgow.

The novelist and poet Robert Louis Stevenson is born in Edinburgh. His grandfather, the notable lighthouse builder, dies the same year.

The foundation stone of The National Gallery of Scotland, designed by William Henry Playfair (1790-1857), is laid by Prince Albert. (The Gallery later opens to the public in 1859.)

1852 Robert Cunningham Graham is born. The son of a Scottish laird, he goes on to organise the Scottish Labour Party with Kier Hardie.

Sir William Ramsay, the chemist, is born. He is later credited with being mostly responsible for the discovery of helium, amongst other rare gases.

1854 The extraordinary Captain Roderick Barclay Allardice dies. A keen walker (slight understatement), Allardice would twice a week walk 51 miles to Turriff, cover a further 20 miles exercising his pack of hounds and then walk 51 miles back home. He was not an inventor, or we would have had the pedometer a lot earlier than we did.

David Dunbar Buick is born at 26 Green Street, Arbroath. He emigrates to the USA with his parents at the age of two. Although he is the founder of the Buick Manufacturing Company (later General Motors), William C. Durant is the person responsible for the growth of the company.

Lord Henry Cockburn, the judge, dies.

1855 David Livingstone reaches Victoria Falls in Africa.

1856 Keir Hardie, coal miner and founder of the Labour Party, is born. His views on Celtic customs: 'I think it could be shown that the position of women, as of most other things, has always been better, nearer to equality, with man, in Celtic, than non-Celtic, races.'

Dr. William McEwan sets up his Fountain Brewery in Edinburgh. Most widely known perhaps for McEwan's Export beer.

1859 Kenneth Grahame, author of The Wind in the Willows, is born in Edinburgh.

The National Gallery of Scotland opens in Edinburgh.

Sir Arthur Conan Doyle, the novelist and author of the Sherlock Holmes mysteries, is born in Edinburgh. He notes, in A Scandal in Bohemia, 1891, 'It is a capital mistake to theorize before one has data. Insensibly one begins to twist facts to suit theories, instead of theories to suit facts.'

1860 J.M. Barrie, the playwright and novelist, is born. Best known for Peter Pan.

1861 David Cooper Thomson, the publisher, is born. D.C. Thomson later becomes Scotland's biggest media organisation, with titles like People's

Friend and The Sunday Post.

Allan Pinkerton, the Glasgow-born detective, foils an assassination plot in Baltimore, whilst guarding Abraham Lincoln on his way to his inauguration.

The one o'clock gun is fired from Edinburgh Castle for the first time.

1866 James Ramsay MacDonald, the first Labour Prime Minister of UK, is born.

1867 The poet Alexander Smith dies.

Scotland's first football club, Queen's Park, is formed.

1868 The last fully public hanging in Scotland takes place – that of Joseph Bell at Perth.

The artist, architect and designer Charles Rennie Mackintosh is born. In Seemliness, in 1902, he says, 'Don't meddle with other people's ideas when you have all the work cut out of you in trying to express your own.'

The Scottish Reform Act is passed giving the vote to all male householders.

George Baxter borrows £100.00 from an uncle and other relatives and opens a small grocery shop in Fochabers. This is the start of the Baxter's food empire.

1869 Edinburgh University becomes the first in Britain to allow women to study medicine (though not graduate). But a woman's cunning plan – to masquerade as a certain Dr. James Barry – pays off, enabling her to get a medical degree at Edinburgh University in 1812 and become an army surgeon.

The 220-foot high Wallace monument on the Abbey Craig near Stirling is completed. It has taken eight years to construct, at a cost of over £10,000, funded by subscriptions.

1870 The entertainer Sir Harry Lauder is born.

Dr Alister Mackenzie, the golf course designer, is born; he is responsible for Augusta National and Cypress Point, among others.

Hector Munro is born, better known by the pseudonym Saki which he uses to write short stories.

1871 The first Rugby International is played between Scotland and England, at Raeburn Place. Each team had 20 players. Scotland wins!

The journalist Henry M. Stanley finds the missing Scottish missionary David Livingstone, with the alleged classic opener, 'Dr Livingstone, I presume?'

1872 Greyfriars Bobby dies after staying by his master's grave for 14 years.

The world's first international football (soccer) match takes place, Scotland v. England at West of Scotland Cricket Ground. The result is 0-0.

1873 The Scottish Football Association is founded. The initial clubs were Queen's Park, Clydesdale, Vale of Leven, Dumbreck, Third Lanark, Eastern, Granville and Kilmarnock.

The missionary and explorer David Livingstone dies.

The statue to Greyfriars Bobby is unveiled.

The Queen's Own Cameron Highlanders is formed – an amalgamation of the 72nd Highlanders, the 78th Highlanders and the 79th Cameron Highlanders.

1874 The remains of David Livingstone are interred in Westminster Abbey.

1875 John Buchan, the writer and statesman, is born in Perth. He becomes best known for The 39 Steps. As well as a writer he also becomes a Member of Parliament and Governor General of Canada. He dies in 1940.

1876 Alexander Graham Bell patents the telephone (Patent 174461). Two hours after it is lodged, his rival, Elisha Gray, applies for a similar patent. Bell's is granted.

The first Scotland v. Wales football international takes place. Scotland wins 4-0. Of course.

Seven Scots, including John Stuart Forbes, are in the US 7th Cavalry with General Custer at the Battle of the Little Big Horn.

1878 The first Tay Rail Bridge opens.

1879 The Tay Bridge Disaster (the bridge collapses during a storm, taking a train with it. An enquiry reveals corners were cut during construction to reduce costs).

1880 Dr Marie Stopes, the founder of first modern birth control clinic, is born Edinburgh.

1881 The writer and historian Thomas Carlyle dies in London.

Sir Alexander Fleming, the bacteriologist and discoverer of penicillin is born. A remedy for a cold ascribed to him: 'A good gulp of whisky at bedtime – it's not very scientific, but it helps.'

1883 The author Compton Mackenzie (Whisky Galore, etc.) is born.

1884 Lord Emmanuel Shinwell, the Labour politician, is born. He is to become the Chairman of the Labour Party and write the manifesto that secures Labour the general election win in 1945.

1885 The Scottish Office is created as part of the Whitehall government (including the post of Secreary of State for Scotland).

1887 The poet and critic Edwin Muir is born.

The new Tay Rail Bridge opens.

1888 John Logie Baird, the television pioneer, is born. A definition of television ascribed to him is

'Seeing by wireless'.

The inventor John Boyd Dunlop from Ayrshire patents pneumatic bicycle tyres.

Glasgow Celtic Football Club is founded, to alleviate poverty in the city's East End parishes.

1889 The National Portrait Gallery for Scotland opens in Edinburgh.

Lord Reith, the engineer and broadcasting pioneer, is born. He is later to become the first general manager of the BBC.

1890 The Forth Rail Bridge opens, having taken six years to build. Its sheer size gives birth to the expression, many years later, 'It's like painting the Forth Bridge' – referring to something that is never-ending; by the time you've finished, you need to start all over again.

Thomas Tunnock pays £80.00 for a shop in

Uddingston. Later on the company produces caramel wafers, snowballs, caramel logs and teacakes that are exported all over the world.

1891 The first Sherlock Holmes story by the Edinburgh-born author Arthur Conan Doyle is published in Strand magazine.

Buffalo Bill's Wild West Show opens in the East End Exhibition Buildings, Duke Street, Glasgow.

1892 Lanarkshire-born James Keir Hardie becomes the first socialist to win a seat in the UK Parliament.

The author, poet, nationalist and socialist, Christopher Grieve (pseudonym Hugh MacDiarmid) is born. He later becomes a founder of the Scottish National Party.

1893 Keir Hardie founds the Independent Labour Party.

1894 The author Robert Louis Stevenson dies

in Samoa. He is best known for his works Kidnapped and Treasure Island.

1895 The coldest temperature ever is recorded in Scotland, -27.2C at Braemar.

Isabella Baillie, the Soprano Dame opera star, is born in Hawick.

The east coast express train from London to Aberdeen sets a record time of 10 hours and 21 minutes for the 540 miles.

1896 The Glasgow Subway (AKA The Clockwork Orange – partly due to the film, but more because the carriages are actually orange, with trains running clockwise on one track and anti-clockwise on the other track) opens. It remains the only underground in Scotland.

1897 The Scottish Trades Union Congress is formed.

Ronald Ross, the first Scot to win a Nobel Prize (in 1902) dissects a mosquito and establishes the link with malaria.

The novelist and politician Naomi Mitchison is born in Edinburgh. Her best-known novels are The Conquered (1923), When the Bough Breaks (1924) and Cloud Cuckoo Land (1925).

Buckfast (Buckie) Tonic Wine starts production. This becomes very popular with heavy drinkers for two reasons: the price and high alcohol content mean that Nirvana can be reached for the smallest outlay. Slainte!

1898 The People's Palace on Glasgow Green opens.

The respected poet William Soutar is born. He is inspired from an early stage by Hugh MacDiarmid and writes such works as The Children and Seeds in the Wind: Poems in Scots for Children (1933).

1899 An experiment using electricity to drive Glasgow's tram cars is successful, sounding the end for the 3,000 horses used by the city on its 150 miles of track.

The novelist Eric Linklater is born in Wales, but ends up spending so much of his childhood in Orkney he considers himself an Orcadian. His wide-ranging works include the satirical Juan in America, the Viking saga The Men of Ness, the two biblical titles Judas and Husband of Delilah, as well as the anti-war comedy Private Angelo.

William Denny at Dumbarton launches the steam ship Sir Walter Scott. The ship is still sailing on Loch Katrine in Perthshire, some 100 years later.

Rangers hold the first match at their new Ibrox stadium. It is a 3-1 victory over Hearts in the Inter-City League.

1900

1900 Elizabeth Bowes Lyon, the future Queen Elizabeth, the Queen Mother, is born.

1901 The Scottish-born Hubert Cecil Booth patents his design for a vacuum cleaner, which sucks in the dust and retains it by means of a filter.

Scotland's other national drink – Irn Bru – is first produced.

Queen Victoria dies and Edward VII becomes King.

1902 Rudolf Bing, co-founder of the Edinburgh Festival and Director 1947-49 (and general manager of the New York Metropolitan Opera) is born.

Edinburgh's Balmoral Hotel opens its doors for the first time.

William McGonagall dies. He has become very famous for writing bad verse. Here is an example:

> And the blankets and sheets
> Were white and clean
> And most beautiful to be seen
> And I'm sure would have pleased
> Lord Aberdeen!

1903 Aberdeen Football Club is founded.

The floral clock in Princes Street Gardens, Edinburgh, begins operation – driven by clockwork and with only an hour hand. But it was the first of its kind in the world! So that's ok.

Lord Home of the Hirsel, later Foreign Secretary and UK Prime Minister, is born.

Hampden Park stadium opens in Glasgow as the home of Queen's Park Football Club.

1904 J.M. Barrie's play Peter Pan is premiered at the Duke of York Theatre, London.

1907 Dudley Dexter Watkins is born in Manchester, England. Although not a Scot, Dudley Watkins becomes famous throughout Scotland for his cartoon strip The Broons and Oor Wullie, published in the Sunday Post every week.

1908 Jimmy Shand, the Scottish country-dance bandleader, is born.

Sir Matt Busby, the football player, coach and manager, is born – Manager of Manchester United Football Club 1945-69, winner of the European Cup in 1968.

The Queen Victoria School in Dunblane opens. It is set up for the sons of Scottish sailors and soldiers. A few years later the sons of airmen are admitted, as have girls been more recently.

1911 The poet Sorley MacLean is born.

1912 Lord Joseph Lister, the pioneer of surgery and antiseptic at the University of Glasgow and Glasgow and Edinburgh Royal Infirmaries, dies.

1913 Dr William McEwan, the brewer, dies.

1915 The jazz trombonist George Chisholm is born.

Keir Hardie, the Labour politician, dies.

1916 James Heriot, the author of All Creatures Great and Small is born.

Clocks and watches go forward for one hour as the Daylight Savings Act brings in British Summer Time for the first time.

Conscription to the armed forces begins for the first time.

The author Hector Munro dies in action in France.

The chemist Sir William Ramsay dies.

1917 For the first time Parliament polls – by a majority of 330 – to give votes to women over 30.

1918 WWI ends on the 11th hour of the 11th day of the 11th month.

Provisions are included in the Scottish Education Bill to ensure adequate facilities for teaching Gaelic in Scotland.

The author Muriel Spark is born.

John MacLean, socialist revolutionary, first Soviet Consul in Britain in 1917, honorary president of the first Congress of Soviets, is tried in the High Court for sedition.

1919 The Bloody Friday Riot takes place – a mass rally of 20,000 strikers in Glasgow's George Square repeatedly charged by police.

Alexander Carnegie dies leaving behind the Carnegie Corporation that has to give at least

5% of its value away every year in charitable bequests. From a sum of about $135 million in 1911, it is worth $1.8 billion on 30 September 2003! Carnegie was a unique man and his dream for his wealth to be used to better humanity will go on for as long as humans live on this planet. In Forum, 1886, he says, 'There is an unwritten law among the best workmen: 'Thou shalt not take thy neighbour's job'.'

1921 John Boyd Dunlop, who developed the pneumatic tyre from the design of Robert William Thomson, dies.

The writer George Mackay Brown (AKA The Bard of Orkney) is born. His novel Greenvoe becomes one of the best Scottish novels of all time.

1922 The popular character actor Fulton McKay is born.

Alexander Graham Bell, inventor of the

telephone in 1876, dies rushing to answer the phone. It was a wrong number (probably Elisha Gray – see p.101)!

1923 The steam train the Flying Scotsman goes into service with London and North Eastern Railway (LNER), on the London (King's Cross) to Edinburgh route.

Lady Elizabeth Bowes Lyon marries the Duke of York at Westminster Abbey, the first royal wedding to take place there since 1383. The couple later became King George VI and Queen Elizabeth.

John MacLean, political activist, Marxist, appointed Bolshevik consul for Scotland by Lenin, dies.

1924 The sculptor Eduardo Paolozzi is born in Leith, Edinburgh.

The actor and comedian Rikki Fulton is born in Glasgow. He becomes best known for his double act with Jack Milroy as Francie and Josie and as the Rev. I. M. Jolly in Scotch and Wry.

Eric Liddell (later famous as a result of the film The Chariots of Fire) wins the Olympic 400 metres sprint in Paris.

James Ramsay MacDonald leads the first Labour government.

1926 In January, John Logie Baird gives the world's first demonstration of television, from his London workshop.

The ballet dancer and film star Moira Shearer is born.

The future Queen Elizabeth II is born to the Duke and Duchess of York.

The General Strike takes place – the first in British history.

1927 The singer Kenneth McKellar is born.

1928 All those over the age of 65 receive a state pension for the first time – amounting to ten shillings (50 pence) a week.

Earl Haig, the Commander in Chief of British forces 1915-18, founder of the British Legion, dies.

The actor and comedian Stanley Baxter is born.

John Logie Baird transmits the first colour television.

The broadcaster Sir Alastair Burnet is born.

The announcement of the discovery of penicillin by Ayrshire-born Sir Alexander Fleming is made.

The voting age for women is reduced from 30 to 21, the same as for men.

The architect and designer Charles Rennie Macintosh dies.

1929 The last tramcars run in Perth.

David Dunbar Buick (born in Arbroath in 1854), founder of the Buick Manufacturing Company, which later becomes General Motors, dies in Detroit.

1930 The New Zealand statesman and Prime Minister Sir Thomas Mackenzie dies.

Sir Arthur Conan Doyle, the creator of the Sherlock Holmes, dies.

Princess Margaret, daughter of the future King George VI and Queen Elizabeth, is born at Glamis Castle. She is the first royal princess born in Scotland for 300 years and the last royal birth to be witnessed by the Home Secretary (a tradition started – ours not to ask why! – by Queen Anne in the early 18th century).

Sean Connery is born in Edinburgh. After appearing in a few small film roles he is chosen to play James Bond. A recent poll of the most popular Bonds puts him head and shoulders above the others. A keen golfer, he is also a supporter of the Scottish National Party. In 1988 he wins an Oscar for Best Suporting Role in the film The Untouchables.

1931 Ally MacLeod, the Scotland football manager, is born in Glasgow. He will be long remembered for the disaster of the World Cup in Argentina in 1978.

1933 The story of the Loch Ness monster first appears in the press, starting off a long-running debate on whether or not some gigantic unknown animal or fish inhabits the murky depths of the loch.

1934 Car driving tests are introduced for the first time.

The Scottish National Party is founded with the amalgamation of the National Party of Scotland and the Scottish Party.

1936 King George V dies and is succeeded by King Edward VIII who abdicates 325 days later in order to marry Mrs Simpson.

George VI becomes King.

The cartoon characters The Broons and Oor Wullie appear for the first time. Millions of Scots read their exploits every week in the Sunday Post and it is still going strong today.

1937 Benny Lynch is crowned the world flyweight champion.

A British record attendance at a football match is set when 149,547 watch Scotland play England at Hampden Park, Glasgow. This is a world record until 1950.

The 999 emergency telephone service comes into operation for police, fire, ambulance and coastguards.

Sir J.M. Barrie, the author of Peter Pan, dies.

James Ramsay MacDonald, the first UK Labour Prime Minister, dies aboard the Reina del Pacifico.

1938 Rugby first appears on British television – England v. Scotland at Twickenham in London.

David Steel, Lord Steel of Aikwood, politician and a leader of the Liberal party, is born. He is elected Presiding Officer in the new Scottish Parliament as it opens on 12 May 1999.

The Marquess of Bute sells half the city of Cardiff for £20 million, at that time the biggest-ever British property deal.

John Smith, the politician and leader of the Labour Party, is born at Dalmally, Argyll.

The liner Queen Elizabeth, then the largest passenger ship ever built, is launched at John Brown's shipyard, Clydebank.

1939 Sir Jackie Stewart, three-times world motor

racing champion, is born in Dumbartonshire.

WWII begins.

A German submarine sinks HMS Royal Oak in Orkney with the loss of 810 lives.

The City of Glasgow Fighter Squadron (No. 602) shoots down the first enemy aircraft over Britain after an attack on the River Forth.

The first bombs dropped on British soil in WWII fall on the Shetland Islands.

Jim Baxter, who goes on to become one of Scotland's greatest footballers, is born.

1940 Billy McNeill, a member of Jock Stein's Celtic team, is born.

The rationing of sugar, bacon and butter is introduced.

John Buchan, author of The 39 Steps etc. and diplomat (Governor General of Canada, 1935-

1940) dies in Ottawa.

The footballer Denis Law, later to play for Manchester United and Scotland, is born.

The evacuation of Dunkirk (which began on May 27) is completed. 338,226 soldiers are brought back to the UK by the little ships.

Winston Churchill makes his speech to the country saying, 'We shall defend our island whatever the cost may be. We shall fight on the beaches, we shall fight on the landing grounds, we shall fight in the fields and in the streets. We shall fight in the hills; we shall never surrender.'

1941 Hitler's Deputy Rudolf Hess parachutes from a plane just south of Glasgow. His purpose remains one of the great enigmas of the war and does nothing to help the 'Glasgow's better than Edinburgh' camp.

The SS Politician, loaded with 264,000 bottles of

whisky, runs aground on Eriskay in the Western Isles. Residents salvage much of the cargo.

1942 The jockey Willie Carson is born in Stirling. In 1977 he becomes the first jockey to the Queen.

Billy Connolly is born this year also. He starts work in the shipyards on the Clyde before becoming a folk singer, comedian and fine actor. He has appeared on the Parkinson talk show more times than any other celebrity.

Prince George, the Duke of Kent, brother of King George VI, is killed when his flying boat crashes into Eagle's Rock in Caithness, apparently en route to Iceland.

The actor Tom Conti is born.

Jimmy Johnstone, footballing legend for Celtic, is born.

1944 Sir Alexander Fleming, the discoverer

of penicillin, is knighted and receives the Nobel Prize.

1945 The singer Rod Stewart is born.

Eric Liddell, later of Chariots of Fire fame, winner of 1924 Olympics 400 metres, dies in a Japanese internment camp in China.

Victory-in-Europe day marks the end of WWII in Europe.

The Scottish National Party gains its first electoral victory when it wins the by-election in Motherwell and Wishaw by a majority of 617 votes.

The Labour Party sweeps to victory in the first general election after WWII.

1946 The politician Robin Cook is born.

The first TV licences are issued in Britain, costing £2.00.

John Logie Baird, the television pioneer, dies. He also developed 3D and large-screen television, and patents fibre optics, now used widely around the world.

1947 The first Edinburgh International Festival takes place.

The paddle steamer Waverley is launched from A. & J. Inglis's yard on the Clyde. After providing services on the Firth of Clyde she has been preserved and still takes passengers 'doon the watter' as the oldest sea-going paddle steamer in the world.

1949 Chocolate and sweets are no longer rationed, a measure introduced at the start of WWII. Of course demand is so great that it has to be re-introduced.

1950 Sir Henry Lauder, the entertainer and songwriter, dies.

The actor Robbie Coltrane is born.

Petrol rationing, introduced during WWII, ends.

Scottish Nationalists steal the Stone of Destiny back from Westminster Abbey. (This is Scotland's Coronation Stone, taken by the English in 1296. However uncomfortable, tradition states that all British Monarchs have to be crowned while sitting on it.)

1951 Gordon Brown, the Chancellor of the Exchequer, is born.

The Stone of Destiny, which had been removed from underneath the Coronation Chair by Scottish Nationalists on 25 December 1950, is returned to Westminster Abbey after being found at Arbroath Abbey.

Conservatives wins the General Election with a majority of 26, beginning 13 years of government.

1952 King George VI dies and Queen Elizabeth II

becomes monarch.

Salvador Dali's painting the Christ of St. John of the Cross goes on display in Glasgow's Kelvingrove Art Gallery. There is a public outcry when Dr. Tom Honeyman, the then director of Glasgow's museums and art galleries, spends the city's entire annual purchasing budget (all of £8,000) to obtain the painting.

1953 The Royal Yacht Britannia is launched at John Brown's shipyard, Clydebank.

The Coronation of Queen Elizabeth II takes place.

1954 Food rationing officially ends.

Alex Salmond, leader of the Scottish National Party, is born.

1955 Sir Alexander Fleming, the discoverer of penicillin, dies.

1956 Tramcars stop running in Dundee and Edinburgh.

1958 The golfer Sandy Lyle is born.

The writer Ian Banks is born.

Denis Law becomes the youngest footballer to play for Scotland – aged 18 years and seven months.

Construction begins on the Forth Road Bridge.

1959 The poet and critic Edwin Muir dies.

Prestwick and Renfrew airports in Scotland become the first in the UK to offer duty free goods for sale. Hurray!

Scotland's first nuclear power station opens at Chapelcross in Dumfriesshire.

The Royal Highland Fusiliers regiment is formed by the amalgamation of The Royal Scots Fusiliers and The Highland Light Infantry.

1960 Real Madrid beats Eintracht-Frankfurt 7-3 at Hampden Park, Glasgow, to win the European

Cup for the fifth year in succession.

Elvis Presley touches down at Prestwick airport, his only visit to Scotland.

National Service ends.

The farthing coin (a quarter of an old penny) ceases to be legal tender.

1962 The Scottish Opera is founded.

The trams stop running in Glasgow. Nowhere in Scotland now has trams and we all know now that this was a big mistake.

1963 The Beatles open a five-day tour of Scotland to promote their first single, Love Me Do.

Jim Clark becomes the world's youngest Formula One motor racing champion.

1964 The Queen opens the Forth Road Bridge. At 6,156 feet long and with a centre span of 3,300 feet, it becomes the longest in Europe at that time.

The first stretch of the M8 Motorway between Glasgow and Edinburgh opens.

1965 The Tay Road Bridge opens – for a short time the longest bridge in the world, at just over one mile.

The maximum speed limit of 70 mph is imposed on all roads unless a lower limit in place.

The House of Commons passes the Bill abolishing the death penalty for murder.

1967 Celtic Football Club wins the European Cup beating Inter Milan 2-1 in Lisbon.

Royal charter institutes the University of Stirling.

Scotland beats England at football – the first team after the '66 World Cup to do so, therefore becoming world champions!

1968 The new 5p (shilling) and 10p (two bob) decimal coins are introduced in anticipation of decimalisation (in 1971).

1969 Dudley Dexter Watkins dies at his desk in Dundee. Apart from The Broons and Oor Wullie, Dexter is responsible for much loved characters like Desperate Dan, Lord Snooty and Biffo the Bear.

The Scottish Ballet debuts at the King's Theatre, Glasgow.

1970 The Kingston Bridge over the River Clyde in Glasgow officially opens. At the time, it is the longest bridge in any British city.

1971 Ken Buchanan wins the World Lightweight Boxing Championship.

Decimal currency is introduced, abandoning 12 pennies to a shilling and 20 shillings to a pound.

David Coulthard, the Grand Prix racing

driver, is born.

Lord Boyd Orr, the biologist and Nobel Prize Winner, dies.

The sole remaining gas street lamps in Glasgow are lit for the last time, bringing to an end the age of the leeries, the lamplighters who started in 1718 with oil lamps.

The Royal Scots Dragoon Guards (Carabaniers and Greys) is formed.

Lord Reith, the engineer and broadcasting pioneer, dies.

1972 The liner Queen Elizabeth I, launched at John Brown's shipyard, Clydebank, in 1938, catches fire and sinks in Hong Kong where it was to serve as a floating marine university.

The UK joins the European Common Market (now called the European Union).

Rangers win the European Cup Winners Cup

in Barcelona.

The Beatle Paul McCartney is arrested for possession of marijuana at his farm in the Mull of Kintyre, Scotland.

1973 Neil M. Gunn, the author of The Silver Darlings and many other books and short stories, dies.

Scotland plays Brazil to mark centenary of the Scottish Football Association.

Sir Robert Watson-Watt, the inventor of radar, dies.

1974 Professional football is played on a Sunday for the first time.

Labour wins the General Election with an overall majority of three seats and Harold Wilson becomes Prime Minister.

The writer Eric Linklater dies in Orkney.

1975 The Scottish Daily News, the first workers' cooperative national newspaper is published but six months later ceases publication.

The Local Government (Scotland) Act (1974) comes into force and nine regional, 53 districts and three islands councils replace 430 local authorities.

A referendum is held on British Membership of the European Community. In Scotland the vote is 'Yes' 1,332,286; 'No' 948,039. The turnout is 61%. Only Shetland and Western Isles have majorities against.

The rate of price inflation reaches 25% in the UK.

1976 David Steel (AKA Lord Steel of Aikwood) becomes leader of the Liberal Party.

The Jesuit priest St. John Ogilvie (1579-1615) is canonised.

1977 Scottish Aviation becomes part of

British Aerospace.

Repairs to the pitch at Wembly are estimated at £15,000 – the price of damage caused by fans digging up the pitch after Scotland defeats England 2-1.

1978 The poet and nationalist Christopher Grieve (AKA Hugh MacDiarmid) dies.

Archie Gemmel scores the best World Cup goal ever against Holland.

1979 The Scots vote in favour of Devolution, but fail to reach the required 40% of the population in favour of implementing it.

1981 Bill Shankly, OBE, dies. A winner of five caps for Scotland, he goes on to become the manager of Liverpool. He is particularly remembered for saying, 'Some people believe football is a matter of life and death. I am very disappointed with that attitude. I can assure you it is much, much more important than that.'

A.J. Cronin, the author of Keys of the Kingdom and creator of the British television series Dr. Finlay's Casebook, dies.

1982 Jimmy McGrory dies. With more than 500 goals for Celtic this legend once scored a hatrick for them in three minutes!

The 20p coin comes into circulation.

1983 The TSB bank of Scotland (now Lloyds TSB Scotland) is formed.

The Queen officially opens the Burrell Collection in Glasgow's Pollok Country Park. (The shipping magnate Sir William Burrell had donated the museum's collection to the city nearly 40 years earlier.)

1985 Jock Stein dies at the end of a Wales v. Scotland World Cup decider in Cardiff. Scotland qualifies for the '86 World Cup finals. A big man, Stein is manager of Celtic when they win nine league titles in a row from 1965 to

1974, as well as winning the European Cup in 1967; the first British club to do so.

1987 The novelist Alistair Maclean dies. His books The Guns of Navarone, Ice Station Zebra and Where Eagles Dare have been made into films.

1988 Sandy Lyle becomes the first Scottish (and British) golfer to win the US Masters tournament.

Prince Charles and the Princess of Wales open the Glasgow Garden Festival.

The actor Andrew Cruickshank, well known for the TV series Dr. Finlay's Case Book, dies.

Pan Am's flight 103, on its way to New York, blows up over Lockerbie killing all the passengers and many on the ground.

1989 Thatcher's government introduces the poll tax in Scotland first. Big mistake!

1990 Rab C. Nesbitt, a television programme, is shown for the first time. Starring Gregor Fisher and Elaine C. Smith, it is criticized for showing Scots as lazy drunken wasters. However, most people just thought it was very funny. Get it on DVD while you can!

The actor Gordon Jackson (Tunes of Glory, Prime of Miss Jean Brodie and Upstairs, Downstairs etc.) dies.

The Queen officially inaugurates Glasgow's year as Cultural Capital of Europe.

Scotland beats England 13-7 at Murrayfield to win the rugby Grand Slam.

Stephen Hendry, aged 21, becomes the youngest world snooker champion by beating Jimmy White 18-12 in the final.

British Steel announces the closure of the hot strip mill at Ravenscraig with the loss of 770 jobs.

1991 Liz McColgan wins the World Athletics

Championship 10,000 metres in Tokyo by a margin of 20 seconds. She wins her first marathon in a record time.

1993 Pope John Paul sanctifies John Duns Scotus, the philosopher and theologian.

1994 Sir Walter Scott's Abbotsford home is raided and priceless antiques are stolen.

The Rt. Hon John Smith, leader of the Labour Party, dies.

The photographer Christopher Spurling confesses to a friend that the now famous surgeon's photograph of the Loch Ness monster is a hoax.

1995 James Heriot, the author of All Creatures Great and Small, dies.

Stephen Hendry wins the World Snooker Championship for the fourth time in a row.

Alison Hargreave, a 33-year-old mother of two

from Spean Bridge becomes the first woman to climb Mount Everest solo and without oxygen. (She dies three years later while descending K2, the world's second-highest mountain.)

In the opening game of her Rugby World Cup programme, Scotland defeats the Ivory Coast 89-0. Skipper Gavin Hastings scores a world record 44 points.

The bridge to the Isle of Skye opens to the public, who are not happy about having to pay to use it and make their displeasure known by protests.

The film Braveheart, starring Mel Gibson as William Wallace, opens to critical acclaim.

1996 The poet and novelist George Mackay Brown dies.

The poet Sorley MacLean dies.

The Stone of Destiny, Scotland's Coronation

Stone, is returned from London to Edinburgh
Castle, 700 years after being stolen by King
Edward I of England.

1997 Billy Bremner, who Arsenal and Chelsea thought
too small, dies. With 54 caps for Scotland and
115 goals for Leeds United he certainly proved
them wrong!

The Referendum on Devolution approves the
creation of a new Scottish Parliament by a
substantial majority.

1998 Tartan Day is celebrated, approved by the US
Senate, in recognition of the monumental
achievements and invaluable contributions
made by Scottish Americans.

The Scotland Act 1998 leads to the establishment
of the first Scottish parliament since 1707.

1999 The novelist and politician Naomi Mitchison dies.

An election for the new Scottish Parliament is

held. Results: Labour 56, SNP 35, Conservatives 18, Liberal Democrats 16, Greens 1, Scottish Socialists 1, Independent 1.

The Scottish Parliament convenes for the first time since 1707. Donald Dewar is elected as First Minister of the new Scottish Parliament.

The Scot Paul Lawrie wins the Open Golf Championship at Carnoustie after a three-way play-off against Jean van de Veldt of France and Justin Leonard of the US.

The Dean Gallery opens to house the Paolozzi Gift and part of the Scottish National Gallery of Modern Art's permanent collection, and host exhibitions. Originally designed by Thomas Hamilton in the 1830s as the Dean Orphan Hospital, its recent conversion into a Gallery was undertaken by the architects Terry Farrell and Partners.

2000

2000 Scotland's first First Minister Donald Dewar dies suddenly after a fall on the steps of his official residence in Edinburgh.

The pop superstar Madonna marries the movie-producer Guy Ritchie at Skibo Castle, putting Dornoch and Scotland in the media spotlight.

2001 Henry McLeish resigns as Scotland's First Minister. Jack McConnell is elected.

The footballing legend Jim Baxter dies.

2002 Queen Elizabeth, the Queen Mother, dies at the age of 102.

The all-Scots curling team wins Gold at the Winter Olympics in Salt Lake City, watched by over 5.4 million TV viewers in the small hours of the morning.

The Princess Royal formally opens The Loch Lomond and The Trossachs National Park, Scotland's first national park.

2004 The actress and author Molly Weir dies.

Jimmy Mack, MBE, the high profile broadcaster, dies.

The Krankies have to pull out of performing in Jack and the Beanstalk at the Glasgow Playhouse after Janet Krankie falls off the beanstalk.

The new Scottish Parliament building opens on 7 September, three years late! The estimated final cost is £431m against the original budget of £109m.

The toll to cross the bridge to Skye is lifted and the crossing is now free.

2005 Sir Eduardo Paolozzi, CBE, artist, filmmaker

and sculptor dies.

On 5 May the Labour party is re elected for a record third consecutive term. In Scotland the results are:
Labour – 41 seats
Lib Dems – 11 seats
SNP – 6 seats
Conservatives – 1 seat!

The G8 Summit is held in Scotland in June at the Gleneagles Hotel, Auchterarder.

The Scottish Parliament votes to ban smoking in pubs, restaurants, bars, etc. from 2006.

THE DECLARATION OF ARBROATH

The Declaration of Arbroath
(English Translation)

To the most Holy Father and Lord in Christ, the Lord John, by divine providence Supreme Pontiff of the Holy Roman and Universal Church, his humble and devout sons Duncan, Earl of Fife, Thomas Randolph, Earl of Moray, Lord of Man and of Annandale, Patrick Dunbar, Earl of March, Malise,

Earl of Strathearn, Malcolm, Earl of Lennox, William, Earl of Ross, Magnus, Earl of Caithness and Orkney, and William, Earl of Sutherland; Walter, Steward of Scotland, William Soules, Butler of Scotland, James, Lord of Douglas, Roger Mowbray, David, Lord of Brechin, David Graham, Ingram Umfraville, John Menteith, guardian of the earldom of Menteith, Alexander Fraser, Gilbert Hay, Constable of Scotland, Robert Keith, Marischal of Scotland, Henry St. Clair, John Graham, David Lindsay, William Oliphant, Patrick Graham, John Fenton, William Abernethy, David Wemyss, William Mushet, Fergus of Ardrossan, Eustace Maxwell, William Ramsay, William Mowat, Alan Murray, Donald Campbell, John Cameron, Reginald Cheyne, Alexander Seton, Andrew Leslie, and Alexander Straiton, and the other barons and freeholders and the whole community of the realm of Scotland send all manner of filial reverence, with devout kisses of his blessed feet.

*M*ost Holy Father and Lord, we know and from the chronicles and books of the ancients we find that among other famous nations our own, the Scots, has been graced with widespread renown. They journeyed from Greater Scythia by way of the Tyrrhenian Sea and the Pillars of Hercules, and dwelt for a long course of time in Spain among the most savage tribes, but nowhere could they be subdued by any race, however barbarous. Thence they came, twelve hundred years after the people of Israel crossed the Red Sea, to their home in the west where they still live today. The Britons they first drove out, the Picts they utterly destroyed, and, even though very often assailed by the Norwegians, the Danes and the English, they took possession of that home with many victories and untold efforts; and, as the historians of old time bear witness, they have held it free of all bondage ever since. In their kingdom there have reigned one hundred and thirteen kings of their own royal stock, the line unbroken a single foreigner.

The high qualities and deserts of these people, were they not otherwise manifest, gain glory enough from this: that the King of kings and Lord of lords, our Lord Jesus Christ, after His Passion and Resurrection, called them, even though settled in the uttermost parts of the earth, almost the first to His most holy faith. Nor would He have them confirmed in that faith by merely anyone but by the first of His Apostles -- by calling, though second or third in rank -- the most gentle Saint Andrew, the Blessed Peter's brother, and desired him to keep them under his protection as their patron forever.

The Most Holy Fathers your predecessors gave careful heed to these things and bestowed many favours and numerous privileges on this same kingdom and people, as being the special charge of the Blessed Peter's brother. Thus our nation under their protection did indeed live in freedom and peace up to the time when that mighty prince the King of the English, Edward, the father of the one who reigns today, when our kingdom had no head and our people harboured no malice or *treachery and were then unused to wars or invasions, came in the guise of a friend and ally to harass them as an enemy. The deeds of cruelty, massacre, violence, pillage, arson, imprisoning prelates, burning down monasteries, robbing and killing monks and nuns, and yet other outrages without number which he committed against our people, sparing neither age nor sex, religion nor rank, no one could describe nor fully imagine unless he had seen them with his own eyes.*

But from these countless evils we have been set free, by the help of Him Who though He afflicts yet heals and restores, by our most tireless Prince, King and Lord, the Lord Robert. He, that his people and his heritage might be delivered out of the hands of our enemies, met toil and fatigue, hunger and peril, like another Macabaeus or Joshua and bore them cheerfully. Him, too, divine providence, his right of succession according to or laws and customs which we shall maintain to the death, and the due consent and assent of us all have made our Prince and King. To him, as to the man by whom salvation has been wrought unto our people, we are bound both by law and by his merits that our freedom may be still maintained, and by him, come what may, we mean to stand.

Yet if he should give up what he has begun, and agree to make us or our kingdom subject to the King of England or the English, we should exert ourselves at once to drive him out as our enemy and a subverter of his own rights and ours, and make some other man who was well able to defend us our King; for, as long as but a hundred of us remain alive, never will we on any conditions be brought under English rule. It is in truth not for glory, nor riches, nor honours that we are fighting, but for freedom -- for that alone, which no honest man gives up but with life itself.

Therefore it is, Reverend Father and Lord, that we beseech your Holiness with our most earnest prayers and suppliant hearts, inasmuch as you will in your sincerity and goodness consider all this, that, since with Him Whose Vice-Regent on earth you are there is neither weighing nor distinction of Jew and

Greek, Scotsman or Englishman, you will look with the eyes of a father on the troubles and privation brought by the English upon us and upon the Church of God. May it please you to admonish and exhort the King of the English, who ought to be satisfied with what belongs to him since England used once to beenough for seven kings or more, to leave us Scots in peace, who live in this poor little Scotland, beyond which there is no dwelling-place at all, and covet nothing but our own. We are sincerely willing to do anything for him, having regard to our condition, that we can, to win peace for ourselves.

This truly concerns you, Holy Father, since you see the savagery of the heathen raging against the Christians, as the sins of Christians have indeed deserved, and the frontiers of Christendom being pressedinward every day; and how much it will tarnish your Holiness's memory if (which God forbid) the Church suffers eclipse or scandal in any branch of it during your time, you must perceive. Then rouse the Christian princes who for false reasons pretend *that they cannot go to help of the Holy Land because of wars they have on hand with their neighbours. The real reason that prevents them is that in making war on their smaller neighbours they find quicker profit and weaker resistance. But how cheerfully our Lord the King and we too would go there if the King of the English would leave us in peace, He from Whom nothing is hidden well knows; and we profess and declare it to you as the Vicar of Christ and to all Christendom.*

But if your Holiness puts too much faith in the tales the English tell and will not give sincere belief to all this, nor refrain from favouring them to our prejudice, then the slaughter of bodies, the perdition of souls, and all the other misfortunes that will follow, inflicted by them on us and by us on them, will, we believe, be surely laid by the Most High to your charge.

To conclude, we are and shall ever be, as far as duty calls us, ready to do your will in all things, as obedient sons to you as His Vicar; and to Him as the Supreme King and Judge we commit the maintenance of our cause, csating our cares upon Him and firmly trusting that He will inspire us with courage and bring our enemies to nought.

May the Most High preserve you to his Holy Church in holiness and health and grant you length of days.

Given at the monastery of Arbroath in Scotland on the sixth day of the month of April in the year of grace thirteen hundred and twenty and the fifteenth year of the reign of our King aforesaid.

Endorsed: Letter directed to our Lord the Supreme Pontiff by the community of Scotland.

Additional names written on some of the seal tags: Alexander Lamberton, Edward Keith, John Inchmartin, Thomas Menzies, John Durrant, Thomas Morham (and one illegible).

Not a lot of people know more than one verse
of God Save The Queen. Just as well as verse six
is not very complimentary to us Scots. Never
mind. We never did like singing it anyhow!

GOD SAVE THE KING/QUEEN

First publicly performed in London, 1745

1. God save our gracious Queen,
Long live our noble Queen,
God save the Queen!
Send her victorious,
Happy and glorious,
Long to reign over us;
God save the Queen!

6. Lord grant that Marshal Wade
May by thy mighty aid
Victory bring.
May he sedition hush,
And like a torrent rush,
Rebellious Scots to crush.
God save the king!

AULD LANG SYNE

By Robert Burns
(1759-1796)
Scottish poet

Should auld acquaintance be forgot,
And never brought to mind?
Should auld acquaintance be forgot,
And auld lang syne!

Chorus:
For auld lang syne, my dear,
For auld lang syne.
We'll tak a cup o' kindness yet,
For auld lang syne.

And surely ye'll be your pint stowp!
And surely I'll be mine!
And we'll tak a cup o'kindness yet,
For auld lang syne.

Chorus

We twa hae run about the braes,
And pou'd the gowans fine;
But we've wander'd mony a weary fit,
Sin' auld lang syne.
Chorus

We twa hae paidl'd in the burn,
Frae morning sun till dine;
But seas between us braid hae roar'd
Sin' auld lang syne.
Chorus

And there's a hand, my trusty fere!
And gie's a hand o' thine!
And we'll tak a right gude-willie waught,
For auld lang syne.
Chorus

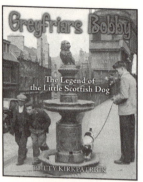

1-905102-04-6
£2.99 available now

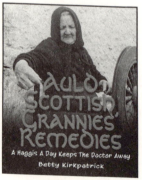

1-905102-06-2
£2.99 available now